THE BLUE BUTTERFLY BETWEEN WORLDS

Poems of Beauty

Alba Bishaj

THE BLUE BUTTERFLY

BETWEEN WORLDS

Poems of Beauty

ALBA BISHAJ

DEDICATED TO

Dedicated to Love.

Dedicated to the Moon.

Dedicated to everyone who is looking for the Truth.

THE BLUE BUTTERFLY
BETWEEN WORLDS

Poems of Beauty

Alba Bishaj

A book for children and adults.

ALBA BISHAJ

From Love. To Love. With Love.

THE BLUE BUTTERFLY
BETWEEN WORLDS
Poems of Beauty

TABLE OF CONTENTS

Introduction

Painting under a full Moon, some colors seemed to be moving my imagination and my heart. Turquoise, white, yellow and violet over my hands. The wings of the Butterfly moved from inside the painting. Maybe I was dreaming, maybe I was creating. A new world in front of me. A new world inside of me. All I wanted was to find the answers to all of my questions. I said yes to changes. I said yes to new beginnings. I needed to breath and feel free, so I went to the water, naked, only some tattoos over my skin. I washed my eyes from all that no longer was good for me. When I came out of the water, I felt free, just like the Blue Butterfly tattoo on my arm.

INSIDE

Conversation With The Moon

Some lights in the sky tonight,
I sit on the ground.
I touch the earth with my feet.
I touch the earth with my heart.

"Dear Moon,
I come to you tonight,
Sitting on the ground,
I don't want to fly.

Dear Moon,
Talk to me.
Tell me about the Sun.
Tell me, how do you feel?"

Hands over the grass,
Hands over my heart,
I didn't know that going deep,
Really means to go up.

My heart is beating tonight,
To the rhythm of earth.
Thank you dear mother,
For giving me birth.

"Tell me dear Moon,
Tell me about your Love,
About the stars and the darkness.
Tell me, do you ever feel lost?"

The Blue Butterfly,
Set next to me.
We are friends.
We are happy and free.

Silence in the air,
The Moon then smiled.

"Are you ready to see,
What really is inside?

The mountains and the water,
The earth and all,
Are made of the same thing,
Are made of Love.

The same Love I feel,
For you, for the stars,
The same Love that makes me,
Shine in the dark.

Love is what I see.
Love is what I spread.
Love is what we all are,
Now and always."

While the Moon talks,
I fall asleep,
Naked and with blue wings,
Truth over my skin."

Paintings

Colors and canvas,
Inside of my room.
Inside my body,
Soul and blue.

"Is this where you live,
Beautiful Butterfly?
Tell me again about Love.
Tell me about your life."

Beating and colors,
Blue, white, yellow and dark,
For there is some darkness,
Even in the light.

Between colors and music,
I feel so alive.
Am I flying?
Am I inside a painting now?

I am looking for the Truth.
I am searching for my soul.
My heart is painting.
In that direction I want to go.

"There you are,
Butterfly full of magic,
How beautiful you look
And somehow so romantic."

Some colors I've never seen before,
Some colors I create.
Is this the real world?
Is this what I paint?

Inside a painting,
Inside a dream,
Inside a book with words.
Inside, how do you feel?

Because inside I find the answers.
Inside I find me.
Truth. Love. Light. Strength.
The colors in here are real.

"Look me in the eyes.
Show me again.
I am ready now,
To know who I really am."

The brush and the paintings,
The colors I create,
The words and the books,

The music and myself.

I am not alone tonight.
I dance between colors and feelings.
"Wait, Blue Butterfly,
Don't go, let's stay here."

"Come with me" she said,
"You were born to fly,
Not just in this painting,
But in the whole world around."

OUTSIDE

In New York

High are these skyscrapers.
I feel a bit small.
I feel excited.
I feel somehow lost.

Big city.
Big dreams.
The world looks different,
Now that I am up here.

Some eyes I see in the streets.
The city looks a bit grey.
Maybe it is searching for its soul,
Between buildings I pray.

Music, noise, light and streets.
Are these the lights I have been looking for?
Silence and freedom.
There is something I miss.

I want to stay over the bridge,
As a symbol of connection,
To what is real and fake,
To what makes us walk and fly again.

New Me,
In New York.
New dreams and new Places,
Here, where there is the new and the old.

In Paris

The Blue Butterfly,
Flew away into another époque,
Surrounded by paintings,
In the city of Love.

It seems nostalgic,
It feels somehow like home,
To fly between museums,
Where time seems to stop.

Colors of another time,
Books and words of poets,
Wings and rivers,
Roses and lovers.

The Blue Butterfly fell in love under the stars,
With the city, with life,
With her true self
And with the night.

We find truth,
In every place we go,
We find parts of ourselves,
Every time we love.

IN BETWEEN

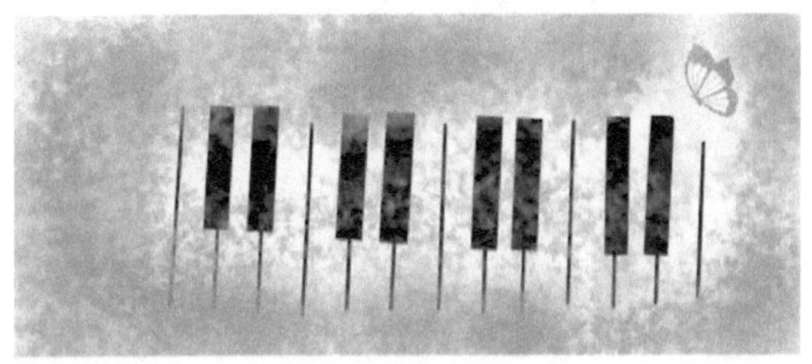

Conversation With The Girl

The girl was painting,
Dancing with the colors.
Moon, silence, Love,
Fingers over the piano.

"So tell me Butterfly,
Where can I find,
What I have been looking for?
Is it inside the heart?"

The Butterfly smiled.
She moved her wings over the piano keyboard.
Even the music seemed lovely,
When she talked.

"There is a secret.
There is truth.
If you listen carefully,
It comes to you.

There is silence,
Between melody and notes.
There is silence,
When I open the wings and when they are closed.

Darkness and light,
They both exist.
Inside and outside,
There is something in between.

Maybe we just need,
To find a balance,
Between what to say and not,
Between letting go and trust.

It is ok to go out.
It is ok to go in.

In the past is what I was.
In the future is what I will be.

But what if we stopped,
For just a moment in between,
In this exact moment,
Breathing in here?

Sit with me now.
Stay with me here,
Between paintings and colors,
Between dreams and real."

Mirrors

I look into my eyes now.
This mirror is so clear.
I close my eyes.
I know what I feel.

I open my eyes again,
Wings blue and white,
"Is this me?
Am I the Blue Butterfly?"

Out of a poem.
Out of a dream.
Out of a book,
In what is real.

Sometimes I fly,
Feeling powerful and loved.
Sometimes I just need,
To connect with the earth and walk.

Mirrors around me,
Mirrors are what I see,
As we all reflect each other,
As we all reflect our wings.

About Fear

"Blue Butterfly,
Sometimes I feel scared.
Sometimes I forget who I am.
Sometimes I feel pain.

Why is it so easy,
To see the beauty and light,
In other people
And forget about my own light?

I am still learning,
Even though deep down I know.
I am still remembering,
Even though I never forgot.

How can I be both,
Strong and weak?
How can I fly so high?
Why do I feel all this so deep?

Is it all about love?
Is it all about freedom?
Is it about creating?
Is it about being?"

The Blue Butterfly,
She came from beautiful places.
She can see underneath.
She knows some secrets.

When she flies in the air,
Blue glowing lights.
Tonight everything is possible,
Surrounded by the stars.

"Look inside" she said,

"Do you believe in magic?
Close your eyes and listen.
The painting brush is yours, just take it.

In the highest mountain,
There is the highest fear,
For you can fall down
And the fall is really deep.

But when up in the mountain,
If you remember about your wings,
They got you up there,
By flying and by the strength within.

If you remember your power,
Up in the highest mountain,
You will not fall.
You will even move the mountain.

Discovering in the end,
That the big mountain,
Was not even real
And fear will have no power.

I deep know,
That life is not about not having fear.
Life is about being brave enough
And learning how to breath.

Looking at the fear,
Right into her eyes,
You will understand,
There is no need to fight.

She is just a protector.
Sometimes she is a liar.
When you become friends,
She burns away like fire."

Photograph

Memories and time,
I look at my pictures and smile.
I was so beautiful,
Even when I was a caterpillar.

Now I embrace,
My memories and who I am,
Because it is the whole story,
Because it is all part of the process.

Pictures on the wall.
Diamonds out of my eyes.
My heart has memory
And knows what all this is about.

The Moon is always the same.
The Moon is always new.
I look at her and ask myself
How can something be so beautiful?

Water and waves,
Under my feet.
The reflection of the Moon,
Over my skin.

I dance with Life tonight.
I dance with these waves.
"Listen to the silence" said the heart.
"Just be yourself.

These pictures you see,
Are not just a reminder of the past.
They are a reminder of your strength
And of how powerful you are.

So take every battle,
Take every fall and fear

And wear them with grace,
As your trophies."

ALBA BISHAJ

LOVE

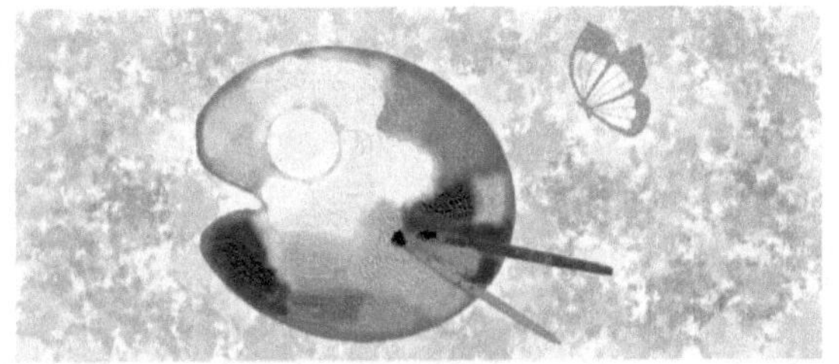

About Love

The Blue Butterfly,
Remembered her grandma' with love,
As a great teacher,
As a warrior.

Life gave her so much joy.
She loved and was loved.
She danced and was so happy,
Beautiful and strong.

Now she became herself a grandma'.
Her heart is full of greatness,
So grateful for life and her loved ones,
Full of love for her nephews.

The time passes.
Some things never change.
Some things like Love.
Some things like the True Self.

Somehow these words,
Will always be here,
To give strength and love,
To all who will read.

Books, paintings, music,
Words, colors and notes,
Are many expressions of me,
Are the expression of Love.

Love, the Eternal,
The Truth, the Real,
The Love we all are,
The Love we all feel.

Tattoo

It was afternoon.
Maybe it was a dream.
The Blue Butterfly flew slowly
And stayed on that grandma's cheek.

"Thank you" they both said,
"For being a mirror and a friend,
During this dreams,
During this whole life until the end.

For there is no end,
We both deep know,
Because we are all made of that wonderful thing:
The Eternal Love."

A little girl walked into the room,
"Grandma', I couldn't sleep,
Can you tell me about that story,
With the blue wings?"

"Come here sweetheart,
You are so lovely.
Sit next to me,
Of course I can tell you the story.

Don't worry about the darkness.
Look how the Moon is shining.
There will always be light,
Don't you worry, my darling.

Now take you favorite book,
"The Blue Butterfly"
And I will read it to you,
In this beautiful night."

The grandma' was reading,
With a lovely and warm voice

And the girl looked at her,
With eyes full of love.

She dreamed and thought
That maybe the Blue Butterfly was real.
She believed in magic.
She felt the Love within.

The house of her grandma',
Was full of books and painting,
Full of pictures and colors.
It felt full of blessings.

"Maybe the wings of the Blue Butterfly,
Are blue as in this painting of grandma'.
Maybe they are like the tattoo,
That she has on her arm."

The girl was so beautiful.
She listened and dreamed.
Deep down she felt,
That the story was real.

One day she would grow up.
She would write her own story.
She would find her own truth.
Blue. Real. Love.

THANK YOU

Thank you to the Heart, for showing the path to us all.
Thank you to the Earth, for teaching us how to walk and be
grounded.
Thank you to the Stars for teaching us how to dream and fly.

With love.
Alba